Holy Family Prayer Book

Prayers for Every Family

MISSIONARIES OF THE HOLY FAMILY

Foreword by Timothy Michael Cardinal Dolan

Liguori
LIGUORI, MISSOURI

Imprimi Potest
28 September 2007
Saint Louis, Missouri
Very Rev. Philip Sosa, MSF
Provincial, North American Province

Imprimatur
9 October 2007
Saint Louis, Missouri
Most Reverend Robert J. Hermann
Auxiliary Bishop of Saint Louis

The Imprimatur is an official declaration that a book or pamphlet is free of doctrinal or moral error. No implication is contained therein that he who has granted the Imprimatur agrees with the content, opinions, or statements.

Published by Liguori Publications
Liguori, Missouri 63057

To order, call 800-325-9521
www.liguori.org

Library of Congress Cataloging-in-Publication Data

Holy Family Missionaries.

   Holy Family prayer book : prayers for every family / Missionaries of the Holy Family. — 1st ed.

     p. cm.

   1. Holy Family Missionaries—Prayers and devotions. 2. Families—Prayers and devotions. I. Title.

   BX2050.H65H65 2012

   242'.802—dc23

                                      2012018445

p ISBN 978-0-7648-2217-9

e ISBN 978-0-7648-6726-2

Liguori Publications, a nonprofit corporation, is an apostolate of The Redemptorists. To learn more about The Redemptorists, visit Redemptorists.com.

Printed in the United States of America

19 18 16 15 14 / 6 5 4 3 2

First Edition

Dedicated to all families of the world

Contents

Foreword

One of my favorite religious communities is the Missionaries of the Holy Family. Founded by Father Jean Berthier, the order is dedicated to the ideals of the Holy Family of Nazareth. They are missionaries in the truest sense of the word, bringing Jesus to all who need to meet him and hear him! One facet of this missionary activity is the pastoral care of families.

The *Holy Family Prayer Book* is a marvelous instrument to help parents and their children strengthen their faith and draw closer to God. The prayers may be well known to many, but they remain ever fresh in their ability to help families imitate more closely Jesus, Mary, and Joseph, the ideal family and model for all.

It has become clear that much needs to be done to strengthen the vocation of marriage and the life of the Christian family. The *Holy Family Prayer Book* deserves a place in every family's home!

TIMOTHY MICHAEL CARDINAL DOLAN
ARCHBISHOP OF NEW YORK

A Brief History of the
Missionaries of the Holy Family

Servant of God Father John Berthier, MS, under the direction of Pope Leo XIII, founded the Missionaries of the Holy Family in Holland in 1895. One hundred years later, in 1995, Blessed Pope John Paul II, in an urgent appeal by letter to the community, wrote of the great need in the world to pastorally care for families. As of 2012, more than 900 Holy Family priests and brothers are serving in 22 countries, emphasizing the Holy Family as the standard of holiness for all families.

Prayer for the Beatification of Father John Berthier and for His Intercession

Father in heaven, you found it fitting to choose your servant, John Berthier, to foster a zealous devotion to Our Lady of LaSalette and the Holy Family of Nazareth and to be an untiring apostle in the education of belated vocations. Please grant me this favor [your intention] so that I may praise you all the more and obtain for myself and others your blessing on this earth and eternal life in heaven.

Grant, O Lord, that John Berthier soon may be privileged with sainthood, in order that he may serve as a model of the virtues he practiced so faithfully during his life. Amen.

For a novena, say one Our Father, Hail Mary, and Glory Be to the Father with this prayer for nine consecutive days.

Anyone receiving special favors through the intercession of Father Berthier, please notify in writing:

VERY REV. FATHER PROVINCIAL, MSF
MISSIONARIES OF THE HOLY FAMILY
3014 OREGON AVENUE • SAINT LOUIS, MISSOURI 63118-1412

Prayers to the Holy Family

Consecration to the Holy Family

O Jesus, our most loving Savior, who deigned to come into the world from heaven, not only to enlighten it by teaching and by your example, and to save it by death, but also to spend the greater part of life in humble obedience to Mary and Joseph in the obscurity of Nazareth, thus sanctifying the home, which was to be the model of all Christian homes: graciously receive this family, which consecrates itself to you this day. Protect us and maintain in us, all through life, your holy fear and love, and true harmony and charity among ourselves, so that we imitate your Holy Family, be one in heart and soul on earth, and obtain eternal happiness and glory with you in heaven.

O Mary, loving Mother of Jesus and our Mother, by your merciful intercession, deign to make this humble dedication acceptable to Jesus Christ, so that we may obtain his grace to be a truly Christian family.

Saint Joseph, guardian and supporter of Jesus and Mary, help us with your powerful prayers in all our corporal and spiritual needs, and especially at the hour of our death, so that we may one day all be united in heaven with you, to praise and love Jesus and Mary forever and ever. Amen.

Holy Family Prayer

Jesus, Son of God and Son of Mary, bless our family. Graciously inspire in us the unity, peace, and mutual love that you found in your own family in the little town of Nazareth.

Mary, Mother of Jesus and our Mother, nourish our family with your faith and your love. Keep us close to your Son, Jesus, in all our sorrows and joys.

Joseph, foster-father to Jesus, guardian and spouse of Mary, keep our family safe from harm. Help us in all times of discouragement or anxiety.

Holy Family of Nazareth, make our family one with you. Help us to be instruments of peace. Grant that love, strengthened by grace, may prove mightier than all the weaknesses and trials through which our families sometimes pass. May we always have God at the center of our hearts and homes until we are all one family, happy and at peace in our true home with you. Amen.

Litany of the Holy Family

Lord, have mercy.

Christ, have mercy.

Lord, have mercy.

Christ, hear us.

Christ, graciously hear us.

God, the Father of heaven, have mercy on us.

God the Son, Redeemer of the world, have mercy on us.

God, the Holy Spirit, have mercy on us.

Holy Trinity, one God, have mercy on us.

("Pray for us" is repeated after each invocation.)

Jesus, Mary, and Joseph…

Jesus, Mary, and Joseph, most worthy of our veneration…

Jesus, Mary, and Joseph, called "The Holy Family" from all time…

Jesus, Mary, and Joseph, father, mother, and Son of the Holy Family…

Jesus, Mary, and Joseph, chaste spouse, pure spouse, and divine Child…

Jesus, Mary, and Joseph, restorers of fallen families…

Jesus, Mary, and Joseph, image of the Blessed Trinity here on earth…

Holy Family, tested by the greatest of difficulties…

Holy Family, with much suffering on the journey to Bethlehem…

Holy Family, without a welcome in Bethlehem…

Holy Family, visited by poor shepherds…

Holy Family, obliged to live in a stable…

Holy Family, praised by the angels…

Holy Family, venerated by the Wise Men from the East…

Holy Family, greeted by the pious Simeon in the Temple…

Holy Family, persecuted and exiled to a foreign country…

Holy Family, hidden and unknown in Nazareth…

Holy Family, faithful in the observance of divine laws…

Holy Family, perfect model of the Christian family…

Holy Family, center of peace and concord…

Holy Family, whose protector is a model of paternal care…

Holy Family, whose mother is a model of maternal diligence…

Holy Family, whose divine Child is a model of filial obedience…

Holy Family, poor in material goods, but rich in divine blessings…

Holy Family, as nothing in the eyes of men, but so great in heaven...

Holy Family, our support in life and our hope in death...

Holy Family, patron and protector of our family...

Jesus, Mary, and Joseph, pray for us!

Lamb of God, who takes away the sins of the world,
    spare us, O Lord.

Lamb of God, who takes away the sins of the world,
    hear us, O Lord.

Lamb of God, who takes away the sins of the world,
    have mercy on us.

Christ, hear us.

Christ, graciously hear us.

Let us pray: O God of infinite goodness and kindness, who has seen fit to call us to this family, give us the grace to venerate Jesus, Mary, and Joseph so that, imitating them in this life, we may enjoy with them the life to come. We ask this through Jesus Christ, our Lord. Amen.

Novena to the Holy Family

Opening Prayer for Each Day

Heavenly Father, your grace reaches us through the hands of your most precious Son, Jesus. His response to the prayers of Mary and Joseph are assured, and so we ask for their prayers during this novena.

Lord, send light to our understanding, inspiration to our decisions, and the fire of pure love to our hearts, so that we will respond to the blessing of your grace in our lives, which comes through the prayers of the Holy Family.

And you, our guardian angels and all the saints in heaven, intercede for us so that we may honor Jesus, Mary, and Joseph by the way we live. Help us to find ways to live as they did and to avoid looking for excuses for not changing our ways.

Father, through this novena in honor of the Holy Family, place in us the desire to pursue and imitate the virtues of the Holy Family and to accept your answer to this novena as your will for our lives. Amen.

The Holy Family: Model for All Families

Pray the Opening Prayer on page 23.

To honor Jesus, Mary, and Joseph is a devotion that is beneficial to all Christians. The lives of the Holy Family on earth serve as models for every state of life for both the individual and the family.

God offers his graces through the Holy Family of Nazareth to encourage devotion and reflection on their lives. We are challenged to make their way of life our way of life.

They are a source of virtue, they enlighten our minds, and they show us how to love through sacrifice. Let us respond to the love they have shown to us.

We pray for a deeper love of the Holy Family.

Pray the Holy Family Prayer on page 17.

The Holy Family: Model of Obedience

Pray the Opening Prayer on page 23.

Mary's acceptance of God's will for her to be the Mother of Jesus began with her saying, "May it be done to me according to your word" (Luke 1:38). With Mary's "yes," the Holy Family began. Joseph planned to divorce Mary until he learned of God's plan for him. And though others did not understand Joseph, he accepted God's will for his life: "When Joseph awoke, he did as the angel of the Lord had commanded him and took his wife into his home" (Matthew 1:24). In the Garden of Gethsemane, Jesus prayed, "Father, if you are willing, take this cup away from me; still, not my will but yours be done" (Luke 22:42). Each member said "Yes" to God's will, knowing their "Yes" required sacrifice, but they had confidence in God's blessings as well. Consider where God is calling us to say "Yes" to his will in our lives. The next time you pray the Our Father, ponder the words, "Thy will be done."

Pray the Holy Family Prayer on page 17.

The Holy Family: Model of Prayer

Pray the Opening Prayer on page 23.

Prayer is a cornerstone of the Holy Family. Jesus, Mary, and Joseph are prayerful as persons and as a family in their practice of the Jewish faith. Joseph and Mary taught Jesus his prayers, and they prayed as a family. They kept the commandments, kept holy the Sabbath and holy days (Luke 2:22–41), and gave thanks for their blessings at mealtime. As parents, grandparents, godparents, aunts and uncles, are we teaching our children how to pray? As children, are we praying for others or only for ourselves? Are we remembering to say grace before our meals at home and when we dine in public? Are we keeping Sundays and days of obligation holy by attending Mass and celebrating family life, or are we instead shopping and doing work that could be done on other days of the week? Consider how Jesus, Mary, and Joseph prayed every day and especially lived their lives on the "Sunday" of their week.

Pray the Holy Family Prayer on page 17.

The Holy Family: Model of Humility

Pray the Opening Prayer on page 23.

Jesus, Mary, and Joseph practiced the virtue of humility to a high degree. Their house, their clothing, and their food were always simple. Humility characterized and directed their work and their ideals.

God resists the proud, but he grants his graces to the humble of heart. (See Matthew 5:4.)

Adopt the way of humility shown in the life of Jesus, Mary, and Joseph.

We should approach the sacrament of reconciliation frequently. Not only do we receive God's mercy in this sacrament, but it also helps us to grow in humility.

By learning this great virtue from the Holy Family, we will live happily and die peacefully.

Pray the Holy Family Prayer on page 17.

FIFTH DAY

The Holy Family: Model of Purity

Pray the Opening Prayer on page 23.

Our Lord said, "Blessed are the clean of heart, for they will see God" (Matthew 5:8).

In the Holy Family, everyone was pure in thought, word, and deed. Jesus is purity itself; Mary is the Blessed Virgin and the Immaculate Mother; Joseph is the most chaste spouse. A person's purity is regularly under assault from the influences of the world, and this was true even in the time of the Holy Family. Pray for a pure heart and for desires that conform with God's will. In addition to prayer, we can help our purity in two ways. First, guard the purity we have today under the protection of the Holy Family—keep it safe from further loss. Consider what we read, watch on TV, or listen to on the radio.

Second, pray that our own words, actions, and attire safeguard and protect the purity of others.

Pray the Holy Family Prayer on page 17.

SIXTH DAY

The Holy Family: Model of Love

Pray the Opening Prayer on page 23.

The love of Jesus, Mary, and Joseph is unconditional and faithful. Without love, holiness of life is impossible. Jesus, Mary, and Joseph are perfect models of pure love, and like all love, it requires sacrifice and forgiveness. (See Luke 2:48–51.) Holy Family, we pray that we can love as you love, and embrace the sacrifice required to love and to forgive when needed. Holy Family, help us to recognize that loving is a choice, an act of the will, and not something we find. Help us to love faithfully and unconditionally, even when love is not returned. As adults, help us to always love the children in our family with our hearts, words, and actions. As children, help us to love and respect our parents. Help us to see and love you, Jesus, in our brothers and sisters, especially in the suffering, the poor, the elderly, and the rejected.

Pray the Holy Family Prayer on page 17.

The Holy Family: Model of Work

Pray the Opening Prayer on page 23.

Prayer and work were the continuous occupations of the Holy Family on earth. By the work of their hands, they earned the bread that nourished them and the clothing they wore. (See Matthew 13:54–56.)

It was the Holy Family who learned to sanctify work inside and outside of the home. Idleness is a source of vice; hence Jesus, Mary, and Joseph avoided it entirely. On the other hand, work can be the seed of virtue.

Holy Family, teach us to make the everyday events of our lives and work into acts of loving God. Teach us to do our work with a Christian heart that will yield our best. Holy Family, help us to see where God wills us to volunteer our time and gifts for serving our brothers and sisters.

Pray the Holy Family Prayer on page 17.

The Holy Family: Model of Trust

Pray the Opening Prayer on page 23.

The Holy Family trusted in God. Mary and Joseph observed the Law of Moses when they presented Jesus in the Temple. As immigrants fleeing from Herod, Joseph followed the will of God and trusted that God would provide. Jesus tells us to trust that our Father will provide. (See Matthew 6:25–34.) By trusting in God and the laws he gives us through Scripture and the Church, we will draw closer to Jesus. How do we trust in God? Do we listen and strive to follow the guidance given to us by Scripture and the Church? Do we accept what is convenient and then ignore what calls us to sacrifice or change? Jesus, Mary, and Joseph, help us to accept, love, and trust in God's will and the Church's teachings, knowing that it is taught for our moral good and salvation. Help us see where we have avoided trusting in God by not following his will or the teachings of the Church.

Pray the Holy Family Prayer on page 17.

NINCTH DAY

The Holy Family: Model of Peace

Pray the Opening Prayer on page 23.

The coming of the Holy Family into the world was the beginning of true and spiritual peace for our hearts. Jesus, Mary, and Joseph, teach us how we can attain peace, namely, by imitating your lives. "For my yoke is easy, and my burden light" (Matthew 11:30) may seem contrary to what we experience. Does living a holy life seem easy or more like a struggle? Our struggle is with our attachment to sin or the desire for material things of this world, not with living as Jesus lived. The more we separate ourselves from sin and material desires and live the virtues of the Holy Family, the more the burden is lifted and the more peaceful our lives become. As you journey with the Holy Family and change your life to be more like theirs, notice those moments of peace and joy. Know that these moments are times of grace from God that encourage us to keep moving in the same direction on our journey.

Pray the Holy Family Prayer on page 17.

HOLY FAMILY PRAYER BOOK

End your novena with an Our Father, Hail Mary, and Glory Be.

Our Father

Our Father, who art in heaven, hallowed be thy name, thy kingdom come, thy will be done on earth as it is in heaven. Give us this day our daily bread, and forgive us our trespasses, as we forgive those who trespass against us; and lead us not into temptation, but deliver us from evil. Amen.

Hail Mary

Hail Mary, full of grace, the Lord is with thee; blessed art thou among women, and blessed is the fruit of thy womb, Jesus. Holy Mary, Mother of God, pray for us sinners, now and at the hour of our death. Amen.

Glory Be

Glory be to the Father, and to the Son, and to the Holy Spirit, as it was in the beginning, is now, and ever shall be, world without end. Amen.

Family Life

Family Morning Offering

O my God, infinitely deserving of love, I love you above all things. Inspired by this love, I offer to you all the actions of this day.

Accept every beat of my heart as a fervent prayer, as an act of perfect love:

- for your sole honor;
- for the conversion of sinners;
- for the perseverance of the just;
- for the deliverance of the holy souls in purgatory;
- for the sanctification of my family and friends;
- for all who have asked for my prayers;
- for those for whom I have a special obligation to pray;
- for the propagation of all pious undertakings, especially within my own family; and
- for deliverance from all evil.

I offer the indulgences that I receive today for the holy souls in purgatory, especially for those within my own family, and for those souls who are forgotten. Amen.

Prayer for Renewing the Family

Holy Family—Jesus, Mary, and Joseph—I give you my heart and my soul. Teach me to live with you in union of mind, of heart, and of soul. Through you, I consecrate myself to the heavenly Father as his docile child. Lead and guide me to live in his love and to accept, as coming from his hand, every sacrifice. All I have I place into your hands for his greater glory, for the renewal and salvation of Christian families, and for the salvation of souls.

Jesus, Mary, and Joseph, help me that my whole future life may be an enduring act of love of God, my heavenly Father. In the union of hearts, yours and mine, may my soul seek and love him in all things. I therefore will not grow tired of invoking your holy names as often as I have a chance during my daily occupations.

Jesus, Mary, and Joseph, your holy names shall ever be present to my mind. They shall supplant every evil or useless thought and shall replace them with the generous desire to imitate your love and self-immolation.

The constant invocation of your holy names shall be a perpetual pleading, so that your love of God and your zeal for souls may be renewed at every moment of my earthly life. May the love you have for the heavenly Father and your zeal for souls be also mine every time I call on you. Aid me never to falter in this endeavor to give to you my whole life. Amen.

Jesus, Mary, and Joseph, I love you! Save souls! Renew the Christian family!

Note: The main purpose of this prayer is to effect in you the readiness to suffer the hardships and difficulties of everyday life in union with the Holy Family and to make of them an offering to God for the salvation and renewal of the Christian family. It should help you to invoke the holy names of Jesus, Mary, and Joseph, and to accept, after their example, all the cares and vicissitudes of life as coming from the hand of our heavenly Father.

This prayer will help you to make it your habit to live in spirit in union with the Holy Family—Jesus, Mary, and Joseph—in your thoughts, in your prayers, in your sufferings, and in your sacrifices in reparation for the enormous guilt of our time.

Your prayer is to obtain from God model parents imbued with the spirit of the Holy Family. Your spirit of sacrifice is to be a seed planted to yield a harvest of many graces for the Christian family, and to foster in them vocations for the priesthood and religious life. Rich indulgences are attached to these pious practices.

PRAYER & NOTE, REV. KARL ASCHENBRENNER, MSF

TRANSLATION, REV. ERNEST BRAUN, MSF

Prayer for Family Protection

O most loving Jesus, who did make holy by your surpassing virtues and the example of your home life the household you chose to live in while on earth, mercifully look down upon this family, whose members, humbly prostrate before you, implore your protection. Remember that we are yours, bound and consecrated to you by a special devotion. Protect us in your mercy; deliver us from danger; help us in our necessities; and impart to us strength to persevere always in the imitation of your Holy Family, so that by serving and loving you faithfully during this mortal life, we may at length give you eternal praise in heaven.

O Mary, dearest Mother, we implore your assistance, knowing that your divine Son will hearken to your petitions. Most glorious patriarch, Saint Joseph, help us with your powerful patronage and place our petitions in Mary's hands, that she may offer them to Jesus Christ. Jesus, Mary, and Joseph, I give you my heart and my soul. Jesus, Mary, and Joseph, assist me in my last agony. Jesus, Mary, and Joseph, may I breathe forth my soul in peace with you. Amen.

Prayer for Missionaries

Holy Family of Nazareth, subjected to various sufferings, obtain
for all priests and religious the grace to endure all things for you,
their holy patrons.

By your poverty, make them detached from everything earthly.

By your flight into Egypt, give them the grace to carry the Gospel
to distant nations.

By your spirit of obedience, teach them submission and reverence.

By your self-denial, obtain for them the grace to conquer themselves.

By your mutual love, make them of one heart and one soul.

By your holy silence, give them true recollection of spirit.

By your union with God, make them zealous for the honor of God
and the salvation of souls.

By your holiness, keep from them all who would not persevere in
a holy life.

Jesus, Mary, and Joseph, enlighten them, help them, and save them!
Amen.

Prayer for Vocations

Loving God and Father of all, we thank you for all that we are and have, and for all that we are able to do. We thank you most of all that, through baptism, we share in your life, and through your Holy Spirit, we are formed with Christ Jesus as your sons and daughters. Dedicated to the Holy Family of Jesus, Mary, and Joseph, we pray that people of our time will be enlightened by the Spirit to discern their particular calling in life.

We pray especially for vocations that respond to the missionary task of the Church and contribute to the evangelization of all for the coming of the kingdom of God.

Awaken within the hearts of many a call to minister as religious sisters or brothers, as deacons or priests, as married couples or as single persons. Grant us all the grace to draw others to the Gospel, to promote vocations, and to commit ourselves to the pastoral care of families.

Jesus, Mary, and Joseph, enlighten us, help us, and save us! Amen.

Family Life
Rosary

The Rosary

The Rosary is a meditation on events in the life of Jesus, Mary, and Joseph.

How to Pray the Rosary

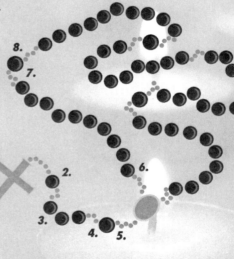

1. Make the Sign of the Cross. Pray the Preparatory Prayer and the Apostles' Creed.
2. Pray the Our Father.
3. Pray three Hail Marys.
4. Pray the Glory Be to the Father and O My Jesus; announce the First Mystery.
5. Pray the Our Father.
6. Pray ten Hail Marys while meditating on the Mystery.
7. Pray the Glory Be and O My Jesus; announce the Second Mystery.
8. Pray the Our Father.
9. Repeat steps 6, 7, and 8, continuing with the Third, Fourth, and Fifth Mysteries.
10. End with the Hail, Holy Queen prayer.

Sign of the Cross

In the name of the Father, and of the Son, and of the Holy Spirit. Amen.

Preparatory Prayer

O God, whose only begotten Son, by his life, death, and resurrection, has purchased for us the rewards of eternal life, grant, we beseech you, that while meditating on these mysteries of the most holy rosary of the Blessed Virgin Mary, we may imitate what they contain and obtain what they promise. Through the same Christ, our Lord. Amen.

Apostles' Creed

I believe in God, the Father almighty, Creator of heaven and earth, and in Jesus Christ, his only Son, our Lord, who was conceived by the Holy Spirit, born of the Virgin Mary, suffered under Pontius Pilate, was crucified, died and was buried; he descended into hell; on the third day he rose again from the dead; he ascended into heaven, and is seated at the right hand of God the Father almighty; from there he will come to judge the living and the dead. I believe in the Holy Spirit, the holy catholic Church, the communion of saints, the forgiveness of sins, the resurrection of the body, and life everlasting. Amen.

Our Father

Our Father, who art in heaven, hallowed be thy name, thy kingdom come, thy will be done on earth as it is in heaven. Give us this day our daily bread, and forgive us our trespasses, as we forgive those who trespass against us; and lead us not into temptation, but deliver us from evil. Amen.

Hail Mary

Hail Mary, full of grace, the Lord is with thee; blessed art thou among women, and blessed is the fruit of thy womb, Jesus. Holy Mary, Mother of God, pray for us sinners, now and at the hour of our death. Amen.

Glory Be

Glory be to the Father, and to the Son, and to the Holy Spirit, as it was in the beginning, is now, and ever shall be, world without end. Amen.

O My Jesus (said after each Glory Be)

O my Jesus, forgive us our sins, save us from the fires of hell. Lead all souls to heaven, especially those most in need of thy mercy.

Joyful Mysteries (MONDAY AND SATURDAY)

The Annunciation (LUKE 1:26–38)
May we be open to the will of God, especially in welcoming an unborn child into our family as a gift from God.

The Visitation (LUKE 1:39–56)
May every expectant mother be a model of trust in God's care for her and her child.

The Nativity (LUKE 2:1–7)
May we always be open to life and choose children over materialism.

The Presentation (LUKE 2:21–40)
May we obey the laws of God and his Church as members of his family.

The Finding of Jesus in the Temple (LUKE 2:41–52)
May we encourage our children to dedicate their lives in service to God.

Luminous Mysteries (THURSDAY)

The Baptism of Jesus in the Jordan (MATTHEW 3:13–17)
May we always be open to the Holy Spirit in fulfilling our baptismal promises as children of God.

The Wedding at Cana (JOHN 2:1–12)
May our Blessed Mother always intercede for every man and woman united as one in marriage.

The Proclamation of the Kingdom and Call to Conversion (MARK 1:14–15)
May we always be open to hear, live, and share Christ's message.

The Transfiguration (LUKE 9:28–36)
May we be transformed and seen as living disciples of Jesus Christ, the Light of the world.

The Institution of the Eucharist (LUKE 22:14–20)
As a family, may we always attend the celebration of the Eucharist with reverence, love, and devotion.

Sorrowful Mysteries (TUESDAY AND FRIDAY)

The Agony in the Garden (MATTHEW 26:36–46)
Let us deal with stress and anger in our lives by relying on God's strength to face and confront our many challenges.

The Scourging at the Pillar (MATTHEW 27:26)
Let us not be afraid to accept the sufferings in life, even if they are painful and seem unbearable.

The Crowning With Thorns (MATTHEW 27:27–30)
As worries of the world grow heavy upon our head, know that Christ is here to help us endure the pain.

The Carrying of the Cross (LUKE 23:26–32)
May we persevere in times of trial and tribulation so that we will never despair.

The Crucifixion (LUKE 23:33–46)
Let us unite our own sacrifices to Jesus for the salvation of the world.

Glorious Mysteries (WEDNESDAY AND SUNDAY)

The Resurrection (JOHN 20:1–18)
May our family be a light and a beacon for the world, so that all will see in us the love of the Risen Christ.

The Ascension (LUKE 24:50–53)
May our family rise above petty disputes and past misunderstandings so that we will live in hope of the life to come.

The Descent of the Holy Spirit (ACTS 2:1–11)
As the Spirit abides in us, may we be faithful in proclaiming the message of Jesus by our lives.

The Assumption of Mary (REVELATION 11:19)
May we, one day, be united with Mother Mary and all our loved ones in the eternal home prepared for us by Jesus.

The Coronation of Mary (REVELATION 12:1)
Faithful to the end, may we be rewarded by Jesus and share in the crown of glory with Mary, our Queen and our Mother.

Hail, Holy Queen (closing rosary prayer)

Hail, holy Queen, Mother of mercy, our life, our sweetness, and our hope! To you do we cry, poor banished children of Eve. To you do we send up our sighs, mourning and weeping in this valley of tears. Turn then, most gracious Advocate, your eyes of mercy towards us; and after this, our exile, show unto us the blessed fruit of your womb, Jesus. O clement, O loving, O sweet Virgin Mary! Pray for us, O Holy Mother of God, that we may be made worthy of the promises of Christ.

Salve, Regina (closing rosary prayer in Latin)

Salve, Regina, Mater misericordiae: vita, dulcedo et spes nostra, salve. Ad te clamamus, exsules, filii Evae. Ad te suspiramus, gementes et flentes in hac lacrimarum valle. Eia ergo, Advocata nostra, illos tuos misericordes oculos ad nos converte. Et Iesum, benedíctum fructum ventris tui, nobis post hoc exsílium ostende. O clemens, O pia, O dulcis Virgo María.

Traditional
Prayers

Act of Contrition

Option A

O my God, I am heartily sorry for having offended you, and I detest all my sins because of your just punishment, but most of all, for having offended you, my God, who are all good and deserving of all my love. I firmly resolve, with the help of your grace, to sin no more and to avoid the near occasions of sin. Amen.

Option B

My God, I am sorry for my sins with all my heart. In choosing to do wrong and failing to do good, I have sinned against you whom I should love above all things. I firmly intend, with your help, to do penance, to sin no more, and to avoid whatever leads me to sin. Our Savior Jesus Christ suffered and died for us. In his name, my God, have mercy. Amen.

Act of Faith

O my God, I firmly believe all the truths that the holy Catholic Church teaches, because you have revealed them, who can neither deceive nor be deceived.

Act of Hope

O my God, relying on your infinite goodness and promises, I hope to obtain pardon of my sins, the help of your grace, and life everlasting, through the merits of Jesus Christ, my Lord and Redeemer.

Act of Love

O my God, I love you with my whole heart and above all things, because you are my loving Father, the supreme and most amiable Good. For your sake, I also love my neighbor, friend or enemy, as myself.

The Angelus

V. *The angel of the Lord declared unto Mary.*

R. *And she conceived of the Holy Spirit.*

Hail Mary...

V. *Behold the handmaid of the Lord.*

R. *May it be done unto me according to your word.*

Hail Mary...

V. *And the Word was made flesh.*

R. *And dwelt among us.*

Hail Mary...

V. *Pray for us, O holy Mother of God.*

R. *That we may be made worthy of the promises of Christ.*

Let us pray:

Pour forth, we beseech you, O Lord, your grace into our hearts that we, to whom the Incarnation of Christ, your Son, was made known by the message of an angel, may, by his passion and cross, be brought to the glory of his resurrection. Through the same Christ, our Lord. Amen.

Queen of Heaven

(Prayed in place of the Angelus during the Easter Season.)

V. *Queen of heaven, rejoice! Alleluia.*

R. *For the Son whom you were privileged to bear. Alleluia.*

V. *Has risen as he said. Alleluia.*

R. *Pray to God for us. Alleluia.*

V. *Rejoice and be glad, O Virgin Mary. Alleluia.*

R. *For the Lord is truly risen. Alleluia.*

Let us pray:
O God, it was by the Resurrection of your Son, our Lord Jesus Christ, that you brought joy to the world.

Grant that through the intercession of the Virgin Mary, his Mother, we may attain the joy of eternal life. We ask this through Christ, our Lord. Amen.

The *Memorare*

Remember, O most gracious Virgin Mary, that never was it known that anyone who fled to your protection, implored your help, or sought your intercession was left unaided. Inspired by this confidence, I fly unto you, O Virgin of virgins, my Mother! To you I come, before you I stand, sinful and sorrowful. O Mother of the Word Incarnate, despise not my petitions, but in your mercy hear and answer me. Amen.

Way of the Cross

Opening Prayer

Almighty and merciful God, who has made the Way of the Cross of your beloved Son a way of grace for us, grant, we beseech you, that while we follow the footsteps of your Son in union with his sorrowful Mother, we may participate in the merits of his passion on behalf of the souls of the faithful departed.

At the same time we offer up this Way of the Cross for the conversion of nonbelievers, heretics, and sinners. Amen.

Note: All Bible verses for the Way of the Cross are referenced from the *Douay-Rheims Catholic Bible* (DRB).

Station I

Jesus Is Condemned to Death

V. *We adore you, O Lord Jesus Christ, and bless you.*

R. *Because by your holy cross you have redeemed the world.*

My Jesus, often have I signed your death warrant by my sins; save me by your death from death eternal, which I have so often deserved.

V. *He did not revile when he was reviled, he threatened not when he suffered.*

R. *But delivered himself to him that judged him unjustly. (1 Peter 2:23)*

V. *Lord Jesus crucified, have mercy on us and help the poor souls in purgatory.*

R. *Holy Mother, pierce me through; in my heart each wound renew of my Savior crucified.*

Jesus Is Made to Bear His Cross

V. *We adore you, O Lord Jesus Christ, and bless you.*

R. *Because by your holy cross you have redeemed the world.*

My Jesus, who by your own will did take upon yourself the most heavy cross I made for you by my sins, oh, make me feel their heavy weight, and weep for them ever while I live.

V. *He has borne our infirmities.*

R. *And has carried our sorrows. (Isaiah 53:4)*

V. *Lord Jesus crucified, have mercy on us and help the poor souls in purgatory.*

R. *Holy Mother, pierce me through; in my heart each wound renew of my Savior crucified.*

Station III

Jesus Falls the First Time

V. *We adore you, O Lord Jesus Christ, and bless you.*

R. *Because by your holy cross you have redeemed the world.*

My Jesus, the heavy burden of my sins is on you, and bears you down beneath the cross. I loathe them, I detest them; I call on you to pardon them; may your grace aid me never more to commit them.

V. *We have thought him as it were a leper, and as one struck by God and afflicted.*

R. *But he was wounded for our iniquities and bruised for our sins. (Isaiah 53:4–5)*

V. *Lord Jesus crucified, have mercy on us and help the poor souls in purgatory.*

R. *Holy Mother, pierce me through; in my heart each wound renew of my Savior crucified.*

Station IV

Jesus Meets His Afflicted Mother

V. *We adore you, O Lord Jesus Christ, and bless you.*

R. *Because by your holy cross you have redeemed the world.*

Jesus most suffering, Mary, Mother most sorrowful, if, by my sins, I caused you pain and anguish in the past, I pray that with God's assisting grace it shall be so no more; rather, be you, my love, henceforth till death.

V. *Love is strong as death.*

R. *Many waters of affliction cannot quench charity. (Canticle of Canticles 8:6–7)*

V. *Lord Jesus crucified, have mercy on us and help the poor souls in purgatory.*

R. *Holy Mother, pierce me through; in my heart each wound renew of my Savior crucified.*

Station V

Simon of Cyrene Helps Jesus Carry the Cross

V. *We adore you, O Lord Jesus Christ, and bless you.*

R. *Because by your holy cross you have redeemed the world.*

My Jesus, blessed was he who aided you to bear the cross. Blessed, too, shall I be if I aid you to bear the cross by patiently bowing my neck to the crosses you shall send me during life. My Jesus, give me the grace to do so.

V. *Whoever will follow me, let him deny himself.*

R. *Let him take up his cross and follow me. (Mark 8:34)*

V. *Lord Jesus crucified, have mercy on us and help the poor souls in purgatory.*

R. *Holy Mother, pierce me through; in my heart each wound renew of my Savior crucified.*

Station VI

Veronica Wipes the Face of Jesus

V. *We adore you, O Lord Jesus Christ, and bless you.*

R. *Because by your holy cross you have redeemed the world.*

My Jesus, who willed to print your sacred face upon the cloth with which Veronica wiped the sweat from your brow, print deeply in my soul, I pray you, the undying memory of your bitter pains.

V. *Turn not away your face from us.*

R. *And decline not in your wrath from your servants. (Psalms 26:9)*

V. *Lord Jesus crucified, have mercy on us and help the poor souls in purgatory.*

R. *Holy Mother, pierce me through; in my heart each wound renew of my Savior crucified.*

Station VII

Jesus Falls the Second Time

V. *We adore you, O Lord Jesus Christ, and bless you.*

R. *Because by your holy cross you have redeemed the world.*

My Jesus, often have I sinned and often, by sin, beaten you to the ground beneath the cross. Help me to use the efficacious means of grace that I may never fall again.

V. *I am a worm and no man.*

R. *The reproach of men and the outcast of the people. (Psalms 21:7)*

V. *Lord Jesus crucified, have mercy on us and help the poor souls in purgatory.*

R. *Holy Mother, pierce me through; in my heart each wound renew of my Savior crucified.*

Station VIII

Jesus Speaks to the Women of Jerusalem

V. *We adore you, O Lord Jesus Christ, and bless you.*

R. *Because by your holy cross you have redeemed the world.*

My Jesus, who comforted the pious women of Jerusalem who wept to see you bruised and torn, comfort my soul with your tender pity, for in your pity lies my trust. May my heart ever answer yours.

V. *Weep not over me.*

R. *But weep for yourselves and for your children. (Luke 23:28)*

V. *Lord Jesus crucified, have mercy on us and help the poor souls in purgatory.*

R. *Holy Mother, pierce me through; in my heart each wound renew of my Savior crucified.*

Station IX

Jesus Falls the Third Time

V. *We adore you, O Lord Jesus Christ, and bless you.*

R. *Because by your holy cross you have redeemed the world.*

My Jesus, by all the bitter woes you endured when, for the third time, the heavy cross bowed you to the earth, never, I beseech you, let me fall again into sin. O my Jesus, rather let me die than ever offend you again.

V. *Think upon Jesus that you be not weary.*

R. *For you have not yet resisted unto blood, striving against sin. (Hebrews 12:3–4)*

V. *Lord Jesus crucified, have mercy on us and help the poor souls in purgatory.*

R. *Holy Mother, pierce me through; in my heart each wound renew of my Savior crucified.*

Station X

Jesus Is Stripped of His Garments

V. *We adore you, O Lord Jesus Christ, and bless you.*

R. *Because by your holy cross you have redeemed the world.*

My Jesus, stripped of your garments and drenched with gall, strip me of love for things of earth, and make me loathe all that savors of the world and sin.

V. *Let us cast off the works of darkness.*

R. *Let us walk honestly and put on our Lord Jesus Christ. (Romans 13:12–14)*

V. *Lord Jesus crucified, have mercy on us and help the poor souls in purgatory.*

R. *Holy Mother, pierce me through; in my heart each wound renew of my Savior crucified.*

Station XI

Jesus Is Nailed to the Cross

V. *We adore you, O Lord Jesus Christ, and bless you.*

R. *Because by your holy cross you have redeemed the world.*

My Jesus, by your agony when the cruel nails pierced your tender hands and feet and fixed them to the cross, make me crucify my flesh by Christian penance.

V. *They have pierced my hands and feet.*

R. *And have numbered all my bones. (Psalms 21:17–18)*

V. *Lord Jesus crucified, have mercy on us and help the poor souls in purgatory.*

R. *Holy Mother, pierce me through; in my heart each wound renew of my Savior crucified.*

Station XII

Jesus Dies on the Cross

V. *We adore you, O Lord Jesus Christ, and bless you.*

R. *Because by your holy cross you have redeemed the world.*

My Jesus, three hours did you hang in agony and then die for me; let me die before I sin, and if I live, live for your love and faithful service.

V. *He became obedient unto death.*

R. *Even to the death of the cross. (Philippians 2:8)*

V. *Lord Jesus crucified, have mercy on us and help the poor souls in purgatory.*

R. *Holy Mother, pierce me through; in my heart each wound renew of my Savior crucified.*

Station XIII

Jesus Is Taken Down From the Cross

V. *We adore you, O Lord Jesus Christ, and bless you.*

R. *Because by your holy cross you have redeemed the world.*

O Mary, Mother most sorrowful, the sword of grief pierced your soul when you saw Jesus lying lifeless on your bosom; obtain for me hatred of sin, because sin slew your Son and wounded your own heart, and the grace to live a Christian life and save my soul.

V. *O you that pass by the way, attend and see.*

R. *If there be any sorrow like mine. (Lamentations 1:12)*

V. *Lord Jesus crucified, have mercy on us and help the poor souls in purgatory.*

R. *Holy Mother, pierce me through, in my heart each wound renew of my Savior crucified.*

Station XIV

Jesus Is Placed in the Sepulcher

V. *We adore you, O Lord Jesus Christ, and bless you.*

R. *Because by your holy cross you have redeemed the world.*

My Jesus, beside your body in the tomb, I, too, would lie dead; but if I live, let it be for you, so as one day to enjoy with you in heaven the fruits of your passion and bitter death.

V. *Also my flesh shall rest in hope.*

R. *For you will not give your holy one to see corruption. (Psalms 15:9–10)*

V. *Lord Jesus crucified, have mercy on us and help the poor souls in purgatory.*

R. *Holy Mother, pierce me through; in my heart each wound renew of my Savior crucified.*

Station XV

The Resurrection

V. *We adore you, O Lord Jesus Christ, and bless you.*

R. *Because by your holy cross you have redeemed the world.*

My Jesus, through your victory over death you opened for us the way to eternal life; grant that as we celebrate your resurrection, we may be renewed by your Holy Spirit.

V. *The Lord, our all-powerful God, is king.*

R. *Let us rejoice, sing praise, and give him glory. (Revelation 19:6–7)*

V. *Lord Jesus crucified, have mercy on us and help the poor souls in purgatory.*

R. *Holy Mother, pierce me through; in my heart each wound renew of my Savior crucified.*

Concluding Prayer

O God, who by the precious blood of your only begotten Son, sanctified the standard of the cross, grant, we beseech you, that all those who rejoice in the glory of the same holy cross, may feel everywhere the gladness of your sovereign protection, through the same Christ, our Lord. Amen. Most loving Savior and Shepherd of our souls, who has given your life for your sheep and has said, "When I shall be lifted up from the earth, I will draw all things to myself," fulfill your almighty word and draw to you all who do not yet know and love you. Graciously look down upon your holy Church, this vineyard, which your right hand has planted; guide and multiply her members, banish all heresies and schisms, and keep shepherds and flock in love and unity.

Give peace and concord to all nations; give the grace of your light to unbelievers and heretics; grant perseverance to the just; and the grace of conversion to sinners. Bless our family, support those who are in their last agony, and grant eternal rest to the faithful departed. Amen.

Prayers to the
Saints

Prayer to Mary: Heart of the Holy Family & Queen of Saints

(Lived before and after the birth of Christ, exact years unknown; feast day, January 1)

Dear Mary, Mother of God and my mother, you had an extraordinary role to play in the Incarnation of the Second Person of the Blessed Trinity, your Son, Jesus Christ. You were the heart in the home of the Holy Family, where you were more of a mother than a queen, caring daily for the needs of Jesus and Saint Joseph.

Teach me to take time, like you did, to reflect on the moments of God's grace in my life, pondering them in my heart. Help me to see how important it is to go to Jesus in the sacrament of reconciliation on a regular basis and to take time each day to pray. Since you are the Queen of Saints, intercede for me to the King of Saints, Jesus Christ, and assist me in my efforts to become a better Christian. Amen.

Mary, Heart of the Holy Family and Queen of Saints, pray for us!

Prayer to Our Lady of Guadalupe

(Appeared to Saint Juan Diego four times in 1531; feast day, December 12)

Our Lady of Guadalupe, Mystical Rose, intercede for the holy Church, protect the Sovereign Pontiff, and help all those who invoke you in their needs.

Since you are the true Virgin Mary and Mother of God, ask of your divine Son the grace of constancy that we may remain faithful in the challenges of life, the grace of fervent charity, and the grace of final perseverance. Amen.

Our Lady of Guadalupe, pray for us!

Prayer to Our Lady of San Juan de los Lagos

(Devotion began in 1623 in Jalisco, Mexico)

Blessed Virgin of San Juan, Mother of God and my mother, the Lord has selected you among all his creatures because he found none as deeply humble as you. Most sweet Lady, in your presence we pour out our poor hearts with all our being. They are covered with hurts and miseries but have great trust in you.

In just pronouncing your name, our souls are filled with hope, and the peace of the Lord brings comfort. Incomparable Mother, remove from us any stain of soul and body. May we abhor impurity. Remove any occasion of offending you so that, being pure and pleasing to the Lord, we may reach the promises of the pure of heart: seeing God in heaven.

Beloved Virgin of San Juan, we pray for our families that nothing be lacking for them and fill them with blessings. Remember us prisoners that beg with love and ask forgiveness for our failures. Amen.

Our Lady of San Juan de los Lagos, pray for us!

Prayer to Saint Joseph: Head of the Holy Family

(Lived before and after the birth of Christ, exact years unknown; feast day, March 19)

Dear Saint Joseph, we honor you as the head and protector of the Holy Family, spouse of Mary, and foster-father of Jesus. Give your just and righteous heart to me as a guide for keeping my soul pure and spotless and free of sin.

Help me to always be an example of purity to my family and friends, especially at home, at school, at work, and at play. May your love and care of Jesus and Mary teach me how to live within my own family, and may we find peace and healing through your prayers. Thank you for showing me that no sacrifice is too great when it comes to my family. Saint Joseph, great carpenter of Nazareth, build a fortress of holiness around every soul. Amen.

Saint Joseph, pray for us!

Prayer to Saint Joseph: Patron of Workers

(Lived before and after the birth of Christ, exact years unknown; feast day, May 1)

Saint Joseph, you were the man closest to Jesus while he was here on earth. You presided over the events of his infancy, and your labors provided food and shelter for the Creator of the universe. You offered him and Mary love and unselfish devotion. No spoken word of yours has ever been recorded; but still the Church, with good reason, cries out, "Go to Joseph!"

O gentle man, who was chosen to be the protector of heaven's most precious treasures, I seek your protection over the lives God has entrusted to my care. Amen.

Saint Joseph, pray for us!

Prayer to Saint Faustina Kowalska: Apostle of Divine Mercy

(1905–1938; feast day, October 5)

Dear Saint Faustina, show me how to love the Holy Family—Jesus, Mary, and Joseph—and in loving them, to love God and every soul he created. Help me to understand how Jesus Christ led you, as his Apostle of Divine Mercy, to proclaim his Divine Mercy message for the whole world, especially for my soul and the souls of all within my family. His Divine Mercy is for everyone, and he has sent his message through you as his secretary.

Inspire me to pray the Divine Mercy Chaplet with my family, especially, if possible, at 3:00 PM, the Hour of Divine Mercy, the hour Jesus died on the cross for my sins and the sins of the world. Mother Mary and Saint Joseph, keep me close to the merciful heart of Jesus, and in doing so, bring honor to the Holy Family as your little apostle of Divine Mercy. Amen.

Saint Faustina, pray for us!

Prayer to Saint Francis of Assisi: Patron of Animals

(1181–1226; feast day, October 4)

Dear Saint Francis of Assisi, give me a heart of concern for all of creation, for all things created by God—every person, the earth, the animals, and all plants—that I may treat them with love and care, just as the Holy Family of Jesus, Mary, and Joseph would do. Help me to be conscious of my environment, the need to conserve earth's resources, and my duties as a good steward.

By your example, I will not be cruel to any living creature, born or unborn. Through your prayers, I desire to fulfill my calling to be a channel of peace to a world torn by violence. Amen.

Saint Francis of Assisi, pray for us!

Prayer to Saint Josephine Bakhita: Patron of Sudan

(1869–1947; feast day, February 8)

Dear Saint Josephine Bakhita, pray to the Holy Family that I will always remain a child of the light. Never let the bitter experiences of my life keep me from doing what is right. You are a shining example of how not to let life's tragedies make me hateful.

You were kidnapped from a wealthy family in Sudan, Africa; sold by slave traders; whipped, beaten, and mutilated by various slave owners; yet you persisted in holiness and became a religious sister. As a sister, you joyfully fulfilled your duties as a cook, doorkeeper, and laundress, even speaking throughout Italy to raise funds for missionary work.

Show me the heights I can reach through Jesus, Mary, and Joseph, and help me never to forget that the choice to be holy, regardless of the circumstances, is always mine. Amen.

Saint Josephine Bakhita, pray for us!

Prayer to Saint Juan Diego: Our Lady's Messenger

(1474–1548; feast day, December 9)

Dear Saint Juan Diego, great lay apostle, on Tepeyac Hill in Mexico City, the Blessed Virgin Mary appeared to you and told you to go to the bishop and ask for a church to be built there. Because the bishop wanted proof, our Lady placed roses, blooming out of season in December, into your tilma, or cloak, to bring to the bishop. We know that the image left on your tilma of our Lady, known as Our Lady of Guadalupe, resulted in the conversion of millions of souls.

Help me to continue to see this miraculous image as a reminder that I am loved by her Son, Jesus. May I also be an instrument of love by bringing hope to those who have no faith, by leading them back to the Church where God's Word, along with devotion to the Holy Family, will enlighten hearts and minds. Amen.

Saint Juan Diego, pray for us!

Prayer to Saint Jude Thaddeus: Patron of Impossible Cases

(Lived during the lifetime of Jesus and one of his twelve Apostles; feast day, October 28)

Saint Jude, glorious apostle, faithful servant, and friend of Jesus, the name of the traitor has been the cause of many to forget, but the Church honors and invokes you as the universal patron of impossible cases. Pray for me who am so miserable; I implore you to use the particular privilege you were granted to provide prompt and visible aid in impossible cases.

Come to me in this great need and allow me to receive the comfort and relief from heaven in all my necessities, tribulations, and sufferings… [here state your petition], and remain to bless God with you and all chosen ones for eternity.

I promise you, blessed Saint Jude Thaddeus, not to forget this great favor, to honor you as my special and powerful patron, and to encourage devotion to you with all my strength. Amen.

Saint Jude, pray for us!

Prayer to Saint Kateri Tekakwitha: Lily of the Mohawks

(1656–1680, first Native-American saint; feast day, July 14)

Dear Saint Kateri, I ask you to give me your faith when facing the hardships of life. Although disfigured by smallpox, you chose to see God and his mercy in everything, especially in caring for children and the elderly. Inspire me to offer my sufferings to Jesus as a prayer for the salvation of souls.

Keep me devoted to praying the rosary, bringing me closer to the Holy Family of Jesus, Mary, and Joseph. Help me to recognize my baptism, as you did yours, as the greatest of gifts from God.

When you became a Christian, you were mistreated, but now you are known as the "Lily of the Mohawks," bringing much honor and joy to Native Americans. Come to my aid so that I, too, will always bring honor and joy to my family and everyone I meet. Amen.

Saint Kateri, pray for us!

Prayer to Saint Maria Goretti: Patron of Purity

(1890–1902; virgin and martyr; feast day, July 6)

Dear Saint Maria Goretti, you are a mirror of the chastity of the Holy Family and a wonderful example of purity and virtue for all young people today, especially those who are tempted to commit sins against their bodies by having sexual relations outside of the marriage sacrament. Help me to refrain from sexual relationships until I marry, because the marital act is sacred and reserved by God exclusively for a man and a woman in marriage.

Rather than submitting to lustful advances, you chose to die in a state of grace instead of engaging in sin. And yet, you forgave your murderer, which eventually led to his conversion of heart and soul. Help me to see that sex outside of marriage is a mortal sin in the eyes of God, and keep me pure and chaste. Amen.

Saint Maria Goretti, pray for us!

Prayer to Saint Martin de Porres:
Patron of the Poor

....

*(1579–1639; patron of people of mixed race; feast day,
November 3)*

Blessed Saint Martin, always compassionate, father of the poor and
needy, look upon us with mercy and pray for us who invoke you
with absolute faith in your goodness and power. Do not forget about
us before God, whom you always served and adored. We bless the
Lord for the great power he felt you worthy to have.

Encouraged by the generosity with which you spread God's gifts,
we turn to you with great confidence. All is expected through your
intercession, through the merits of Jesus Christ, our Lord. Amen.

Saint Martin de Porres, pray for us!

Prayer to Saint Maximilian Mary Kolbe: Patron of Prisoners

(1894–1941; priest and martyr; feast day, August 14)

Dear Saint Maximilian Mary Kolbe, please pray to Jesus, Mary, and Joseph for me, and help me to understand what direction my life should take: the single life, the married state, or a religious vocation. Whatever state in life God chooses for me, may I be heroic in serving him. If I am to remain in the single life, let me be holy and chaste; if I am called to marriage, let me be a faithful spouse; and if I am to be a priest, deacon, brother, or sister, let me remain true to my vows.

Like you, never let me count the costs of whatever road I choose in following the example of the Blessed Virgin Mary, the foremost disciple of Jesus Christ. Like you, never let me count the costs in loving friend and foe alike, as you did by dying for your friends in a concentration camp in Nazi Germany. Amen.

Saint Maximilian Mary Kolbe, pray for us!

Prayer to Saint Nicholas: Patron of Children

(?–c. 350; bishop; feast day, December 6)

Dear Saint Nicholas, your extraordinary generosity makes you a wonderful saint for the Advent and Christmas seasons, and that is why you are often remembered as "Santa Claus." Help me to prepare for the coming of Jesus, and to see the sufferings of Mary and Joseph in light of all their difficulties in finding a place for his birth.

Inspire me not to think about the Christmas gifts I will receive, but rather, to think of others and what I can do for them—as you did by giving to others in need, especially at the crucial times when they needed a friend the most. May my life always be a gift to others, especially to my family and the Holy Family. Amen.

Saint Nicholas, pray for us!

Prayer to Saint Teresa of Avila: Doctor of the Church

(1515–1582; feast day, October 15)

Dear Saint Teresa of Avila, with devotion to Jesus, Mary, and Joseph, teach me that, like you, I can be a person of deep prayer and still be active in the world. The Holy Family is a perfect example of living in the world without being part of the world.

You helped reform your religious order of sisters, the Carmelite Order. Help me to reform my life and to be a holy example for those who are members of my everyday life, especially those within my own family. Teach me how to be a person of service to others as I overcome my own sufferings every day without complaining. Amen.

Saint Teresa of Avila, pray for us!

Prayer to Saint Thérèse of Lisieux: The Little Flower

(1873–1897; Doctor of the Church; feast day, October 1)

Dear Saint Thérèse, please help me to honor my parents and others the way Jesus did when he was living with Mary and Joseph here on earth. And show me how to live your "Little Way" in all that I do—that is, doing little things every day with great love for God.

I know that God does not ask great things from me, but he wants me to live each day loving him with all my heart and soul; being kind to all those I meet; caring for the poor and the elderly; and trying to do my very best at everything I do. But most of all, teach me how to love the unlovable so that I may be a rose in their life of thorns.

Your Little Way is so special that Blessed Pope John Paul II proclaimed you a Doctor of the Church. May your Little Way be my way too. Amen.

St. Thérèse, pray for us!

Prayers Before the Blessed Sacrament

The Eternal Last Supper

Dear Jesus, as I pray before you in the Blessed Sacrament and reflect on the Last Supper, the last meal, a Passover supper that you ate with your disciples the night before you died—I meditate on the betrayal of Judas and his deadly kiss, and I think of how many times I have betrayed you with the kiss of my sin.

But what fills my heart with hope is the new Passover, anticipated in the Last Supper and celebrated in the Eucharist at every Mass, which fulfills the Jewish Passover and anticipates the final Passover of the Church in the glory of your kingdom.

Jesus, have mercy on me, a sinner! Amen.

Jesus: "I Thirst" (For You)

Dear Jesus, as I pray before you in the Blessed Sacrament of the altar, I reflect on your crucifixion and all your sufferings for my sins, and I recall your words from Scripture, "I thirst!" for souls (John 19:28–30).

God the Son, through your Incarnation, you fully assumed our weakness in order that we may be delivered from an eternal death of spiritual thirst by partaking of your salvation. When you said the words, "It is finished," the work of salvation for the redemption of sinful humanity is completed with your death, Jesus Christ, on the cross.

Let me never forget the price you paid for my redemption and the redemption of the whole world as I come before you and thank you on behalf of all those who never remember to thank you. Amen.

Mary, Mother of the Eucharist

Dear Mary, Mother of the Eucharist, as I sit here before Jesus Christ in the Blessed Sacrament, which contains his Body, Blood, Soul, and Divinity, and which contains the Holy Trinity, enlighten me in praying to the Holy Trinity since you are the Daughter of the Father, the Mother of the Son, and the Spouse of the Holy Spirit.

No one is closer to the Holy Trinity than you. As I sit here before the divinity of Jesus in the presence of the Holy Trinity—Father, Son, and Holy Spirit—let me spend time in this house of love. It is truly a house of love, for the Holy Spirit is the love of the Father and the Son for each other. Amen.

Joseph, Foster-Father of the Eucharistic Jesus

Dear Saint Joseph, foster-father of the eucharistic Jesus, as I pray before Jesus in the Blessed Sacrament containing his Body, Blood, Soul, and Divinity, I reflect on how God's Son lived within the structure of a family where you were the head and protector of that family. The Holy Family was the earthly trinity, a reflection of the heavenly Trinity. You are the standard of holiness as father and husband, and your strength fills me with peace as I meditate on your Seven Sorrows*:

(1) Finding our Lady had conceived and initially believing that your only option was to "divorce her secretly"; (2) Not finding any lodging in the city of Bethlehem for Mary to give birth; (3) Seeing the divine Infant suffer and shed blood at his circumcision; (4) Hearing the prophecy of Saint Simeon that Jesus would be an object of contradiction and that Mary's own soul would be pierced by a sword; (5) The flight into Egypt to save the Child's life from King Herod; (6) Finding that the cruel Archelaus had succeeded his father, Herod, upon your return from Egypt; and

(7) Losing the Child Jesus for three days when he was twelve years old. Amen.

(*Giovanni de Fano, 1469–1539)

Eucharistic Jesus:
Source and Summit of Family Life

Jesus, I place myself in your eucharistic presence, for you are the true source and summit of all family life. Unfortunately, due to a lack of faith and morality, families today are breaking apart and dishonored by a culture of death: artificial contraception, abortion, adultery, homosexual lifestyles, sexually transmitted diseases, divorce, drugs, pornography, glorified sex and violence, teenage pregnancy, consumerism, and materialism.

I turn to you and meditate on the holiness of your sacred family, and I see what a true family should be, regardless of the daily trials and tribulations: for you were born in poverty in a stable; you had to flee from persecution to Egypt with Mary and Joseph; you grew up working with your hands as a carpenter at the side of your foster-father, Joseph; and the death of Joseph resulted in Mary's becoming a widow.

Give my family the confidence of the Holy Family in all of our sufferings so that we, too, will overcome our difficulties in a spirit of mercy and forgiveness, knowing that the Holy Family is always there to help us. Amen.

Your Invitation to Pray for the Renewal of the Christian Family

In the last quarter century, the Christian family has undergone major disruptions, and it is relentlessly attacked by a Culture of Death.

Who knows better the difficulties and challenges faced by families today than faithful parents and grandparents with their own families, immediate and extended?

Please consider praying for all families by joining the Friends of the Missionaries of the Holy Family Prayer Association.

Contact us the following ways:

Toll-free: 1-888-484-9945
Website: www.MSF-America.org
E-Mail: MSF@MSF-America.org
Mail: 3014 Oregon Avenue · St. Louis, MO 63118

GOD BLESS YOUR FAMILY!